Birds
for a
Demolition

Birds
for a
Demolition

poems by
Manoel de Barros

translated from the Portuguese by
Idra Novey

Carnegie Mellon University Press
Pittsburgh 2010

Acknowledgments

Grateful acknowledgment is made to the National Endowment for the Arts for supporting the completion of this book, to PEN for featuring Barros' work as part of their annual translation feature, and to the journals below where some of these translations first appeared:

BOMB: "The Rock," "Day One, 1," "Day Three," "The Illness," and "Visit"
Circumference: "Small World" and "The Use of Material and Birds for a Demolition"
Denver Quarterly: "Day One, 2," "The Art of Infantilizing Ants," and "Six or Thirteen Things I Learned about Myself"
Guernica: "In War" and section VIII of "An Education on Invention"
Pequod: "Biography of Dew"
Rattapallax: "Job, Anew"
Subtropics: "The Book about Nothing" and "Resigned"
Washington Square: "The Tin Man"
Words Without Borders: "Devotion" and "Song of Seeing"
eXchanges: "Ants" and section II of "Thrush in Darkness"
Zoland Poetry: "Invented Memoir"

Many thanks to Ana Cristina dos Santos for her wonderful insights on these poems and on the Pantanal, and to Flavia Rocha for introducing me to Barros and for her help with "Job, Anew," "Song of Seeing," and "Portrait of the Artist as a Thing."

Book design: Scott F. Rosenfeld

Library of Congress Control Number 2009940930
ISBN 978-0-88748-523-7
Copyright © 2010 by Manoel de Barros
English translation copyright © 2010 by Idra Novey
All rights reserved
Printed and bound in the United States of America

10 9 8 7 6 5 4 3 2 1

Contents

Introduction: Translating the Riverbed	7
Devotion	9

Poems 1960-1982

Visit	13
Job, Anew	14
The Use of Materials and Birds for a Demolition	17
The Tin Man	22
from Thrush in Darkness	26

Poems 1985-1993

Small World	33
Day One	34
Day Two	36
Day Three	38
Six or Thirteen Things I Learned about Myself	40
Portrait	43
An Education on Invention	44

from **The Book about Nothing, 1996**

Ants	53
The Book about Nothing	54
Desiring to Be	59

Poems 1998-2009

In War	77
Of Birds	78
The Rock	79
Portrait of the Artist as a Thing	80

Invented Memoir	81
from Song of Seeing	82
from Biography of Dew	83
The Illness	84
Self-Portrait	85
The Art of Infantilizing Ants	86
The Two	90
Filth	91
Resigned	92
Invented Memoir, II	93
About the Author	94
About the Translator	95

Introduction

Translating the Riverbed

Manoel de Barros didn't charge onto the Brazilian poetry scene. He waded in. When Elizabeth Bishop edited her seminal anthology of Brazilian poetry in 1972, Barros wasn't much known outside the marshy Pantanal region where he was raised. Born in 1916, he had to leave the wetlands to get an education and tried out the life of an urban lawyer but missed the Pantanal, and so, in 1960, he returned to his family's ranch.

For the next twenty years, far from Brazil's predominantly urban poetry world, he went on writing, publishing with small regional presses until the 1980s, when he began to land his country's top awards, several of them twice. By the time Barros won Brazil's prestigious Jabuti Prize for the second time in 2002, his surreal, riveting poems were known throughout Brazil and starting to gain attention abroad. His unusual life and art were also the subject of a film, *O Caramujo Flor*, directed by Joel Pizzini in 1989. Now in his nineties and the author of over twenty-five books, Barros enjoys national recognition as one of the most radical and inventive Brazilian poets of the last hundred years.

In the U.S. what we hear of Brazil is most often the brutal violence taking place in Rio and São Paulo, but Barros writes of the vast rest of the country—the wetlands and rivers the millions of migrants to Brazil's cities are abandoning for the lack of economic opportunities there. In Barros' poems, that migration is a phantom theme. What the reader experiences are the houses those migrants leave behind, the fungi blooming on their walls and the vines taking over their verandas. Barros shows the poverty and solitude of rural life, but also its sensuality and its wealth of geckos, open spaces and butterflies.

In Brazil's *Jornal de Poesia*, the critic Antero Barbosa wrote that what makes Barros' work so distinctive is that his poems "never separate themselves from the riverbeds" of which they speak. In his poems, "it is possible to hear or breathe the words, to feel the precarious condition of the things they signify," as another writer, João Borges, described them in the newspaper *O Estado de Sao Paulo*.

To bring these riverbed-poems into English has been an intense experience. In Paul Auster's novel *Oracle Night*, the main character disappears from his room every time he sits down and writes in a certain blue journal. I experienced a similar sensation each time I sat down to translate these poems. Within minutes, I'd feel like I was no longer in my apartment, but off catching frogs behind a kitchen wall or starting to "exhibit traits of a fruit fly."

In a review of Barros' 2004 book, *Poemas Rupestres*, the critic Ricardo Santhiago wrote that Barros' poetry reads like an archaeology of the future, a poetry that "immediately becomes canonical and everlasting." I hope some of that immediacy comes through in these translations.

At ninety-one-years-old, Barros recently published the third and possibly final volume of his *Invented Memoirs*. I've included several poems from that book in the last section here. That volume, like the two before it, comes in a thin cardboard box that looks like it might contain a silk tie or a silver picture frame. Instead, inside, are pages held together with a ribbon from one of the most gifted living poets in Brazil. "In this regard," he writes, "our life was a caress."

–Idra Novey
New York City, 2010

Devotion

There was a high wall between our houses.
Difficult to send her a message.
There was no email.
Her father was a jaguar.
We tied notes to a rock bound to a rope
and I threw the rock into her backyard.
It was glorious.
But sometimes the note got stuck in the branches of the
    guava tree
and then it was agony.
So it was in the time of jaguars.

1960 - 1982

Visit

In the cell of Pedro Norato, twenty-three years in seclusion,
death naps with its legs open . . .
Between the prison bars it weeds its way in.
It has the blighted sleep of thighs.
Norato told me he found a woman inside a pot then drank her.
It is without love we find ourselves with God, he said.
The world is not perfect like a horse, he told me.
In clocks, he sees long trills of water.
He beats a salute for the flies.

Along the gutters, I go home.

Job, Anew

> Therefore
> How to know things if not by being them?
> *–Jorge de Lima*

Usufruct among creatures,
roots, clay, and water,
a man lived
on a heap of stones.

Inside his landscape
— between stone and himself —
a mollusk grew.

Moss bloomed . . .
Crept up to my lips,
ate around my mouth
leaving a ruined room.

Coexistence of myrtle
and frogs. . . . A mouth of root
and water oozing mud.

It was good
to sleep on a cold and slippery bed
of stones,
to leave everything
on the tip of a dagger.

It was good
to be a creature
that crawls across stones;
to be vegetable root
to be water.

It was good to walk anonymous
in the afternoon
with birds above
and the wind in my yellow clothes.

To never have a place to go.
To never choose anything.
To keep walking, small under the rain
twisted like an apple tree.

It was good to perch afterward
among worn boots . . .
like a dog
a fork forgotten in the sand.

The land receiving me
giving me shelter
using me like a stamp
a shoe
a teapot with no spout.

To be like things that have no mouth!
Communication by infusion
by rite
by incrustation. . . . To be creatures, children,
    dry leaves.

To let fungus grow between the toes.
The rusted flesh,
bird, word, icon, unmade into flowers.
My clothes a kingdom of moths.

It was good
to be like a rush
long in the ground: dry and hollow.
Full of sand, ants, sleep.
To be stone under shade (a meal for mosses)
To be soft fruit on the ground, relinquished
to things . . .

The Use of Materials and Birds for a Demolition

Walk No. 1

  After getting together with Alyosha Karamazoff
I leave behind the dead house
  With my feet, I try to find the little things
on the ground near the ocean
  In my mouth a deafness
  I exhibit traits of the fruit fly

Walk No. 2

A man (lone as a bridge) was seen
from the veranda by a group of fools
   A tree was thickening in his voice
   And his face was a field

Walk No. 3

    Thrush roots and moss
climb up the walls
    It wasn't normal
the lizard feeling he found in the word *walls*

Walk No. 4

    A man spotted himself: his outer side climbing
up a ladder . . .
    Paths the devil didn't knead—he said
    The clock was hours off
He caught a little scrub grass
    invading the ruins of his mouth

Walk No. 5

Hovels in collapse
    cracked walls
And the slug—in its freedom
    to go about naked and damp!

The Tin Man

The tin man
plants trees through a pair of holes
in his face

The tin man
is armed with nails
and has the nature of an eel

The tin man
can be found in the waiting mouth
of corrosion

The tin man
trims himself at the edges
and dies from a lack of birds
in his knees

The tin man
bears across the land
what his grandfather was as a lizard

What his mother was as a stone
and what his house used to be
beneath a stone

The tin man
bears a tin condition
and dies from his tin

The tin man
has the wilted edges of a rose
and is mended by the sun

He dies inside a stone
an example of a thing
that doesn't unsettle a hair

The tin man
begins in thorns
and his eyes rely
on the diversions of birds

On the tin man
a cool slug walls itself in
and falls in the moonlight

To hear the ocean's murmur
the tin man
inscribes himself in the tide

The tin man
is devoured by stone
and by tree

The tin man
is a small vigilant bird
he won't twitter

He's the coarse trunk
on the shoreline
he's the growth of slime
in the mouth

The tin man
seaweeds himself
into the park

The tin man
breaks into a great fit of leaves
and drags himself
in his grassy sounds

Onto the tin man
the frog fastens
his irrigated mouth

The tin man
escapes his tin
in order to stick
and slither

The tin man
walls the smallest
of mollusks inside him

The tin man
comes costumed as a chameleon

The tin man
makes a cut in his mouth
to drain all his silence

The tin man
is anxious
for trees

The tin man
is a perfect case
for lizards

The tin man
is the amphibian remains
of a person

The tin man
is ruined
by butterflies

The tin man
is branded with iron and fire
by the rain

from Thrush in Darkness

I

Meanderer in my swamp,
      I arrive at a thicket of birds.

A man who studied ants and tended to rocks
told me in THE LAST KNOWN RESIDENCE:
      only bother with the futile.

His language was a depository for twisted shadows,
verses covered with ivy and rusted gutters that widen
into a wing over us.

A man was fixed for a thousand years in this place
without ears.

II

                (after a *Pierrot* by Picasso)

Pierrot is an errant unfigure,
an ambler in claret sunsets.
Living from what he desists,
he expresses himself best in insects.

Pierrot has a face of water
that clears with a mask.
His uncolor appears
like a glass face in a pool.

He has his interior variations:
he's addicted to the roots of walls.
His posture possesses years
of the amorphous and deserted.

Pierrot's left side
is affixed to rubble.
And the other side to rubble.
....
Solitude has a cavernous face.

III

Before anything else a poem is an un-utensil.

To begin it's convenient
to be dressed in ratty clothes.

There are those who tinker under a car
in the first seconds.

An open window helps,
a ready vein.

For me a poem is a thing that serves no purpose
while life remains.

Nobody fathers a poem without dying.

1985 - 1993

Small World

My world is small, Lord.
There is a river and a few trees.
The back of our house faces the water.
Ants trim the edge of Grandmother's rose beds.
In the backyard, there is a boy
and his wondrous tin cans.
His eye exaggerates the blue.
Everything from this place has a pact
        with birds.
Here, if the horizon reddens a little,
        the beetles think it's a fire.
Where the river starts a fish,
                river me a thing
River me a frog
River me a tree.
In the evenings, an old man plays his flute
to invert the sunsets.

Day One

1.1

Yesterday it rained in the future.
Water soaked my embarrassments.
My sleepwear.
My set of dishes.
I sail the flood's rise to the image of a cork.
My canoe is light as a stamp.
These waters have no other edge.
From here all I glimpse is the border of the sky.
(Maybe a vulture has his eye on me.)
Today I'm lined up with the cup of the leaves.
Fish eat caranda fruits in the stands of palm trees.

1.2

I know of the egg's illuminations.
Flags don't flutter because of me.
I don't emanate sparkles
or come from noblemen.
Greater than the infinite is the uncolored.
I am my own personal flag.
I need the waste of words to include me.
My emptiness is full of inherences.
In this I have much in common with stones.
....
(What lies at a distance is pre-clear
or simply dark?)

Day Two

2.1

The heart is a place without conduct.
I move along paths divided with others.
I accommodate the clouds in my eye.
The hour's light disproportions me.
I am everything the wind mistreats.
My beacon is a sunset with swallows.
I evolve my state of being until I am alongside a rock.
A drizzle settles over the night.
I accept the evening as fate.
An owl blocks my way
at the end of a darkness.

2.2

Dirtinesses recolor me.
I repose in the water's composure.
It's in the mummy position I place myself.
I won't use theater props.
My fight isn't for facades.
The sky's design unfixes me.
The hyacinth's vigor is my festoon.
Day's end increases my unease.
At times I undergo defoliations.

Like a friar, I'm going to undie of stone.

Day Three

3.1

The moon makes silence for the birds,
             –I hear the rumors!
A red perfume thought me into being.
(Maybe I'm contaminating the twilight.)
These empty considerations restrict me more.
Some pieces of me are already in exile.
....
(Is it good sense that augments absurdity?)
At night I drink water from a packed lunch.
I use the wind for self-maintenance.
I uneat without opulence.
Excuse my delicacy.

3.2

Clouds engulf me from below.
What I have is the ache of an extracted conch.
An ache of pieces that won't return.
I'm various people undone.
………………………………..
………………………………..

At a distance I spot the shoulder of a ship.
And shrugging in the sand a few jabiru.
I get closer and tremble.
I spot the Village of Guanás and pull up
in a rusted can.
                    A thrush hallelujahs me.

Six or Thirteen Things I Learned about Myself

1.

The necktie of a vulture is colorless.
Leaning into the shadow of a lone nail, the vulture is born.
Moonlight on the rooftops flusters the dogs.
Waters crystallize on the leg of a fly.
June bugs don't use their wings when they track over
    excrement.
A poet is a creature who licks words and gets delirious.
In the bone of a lunatic's speech are the lilies.

3.

There are four tree theories I know well.
First: that a shrub of garbage is mightier for its ants.
Second: that a filth plant produces the most flaming fruits.
Third: in vines that strike through the cracks in walls a sensual
    power grows in the cavities.
Fourth: that there are in lone trees a superior rapture for
    horizons.

7.

Intimate is the rain
If seen from a wall damp with flies;
If beetles appear in the foliage;
If geckos stick to the mirrors;
If cigarettes, out of love, get lost in the trees;
And the dark dampens on our skin.

9.

In passing her vaginula over the poor things of the ground,
the slug leaves little liquid prints.
It influences my desire to slobber over words.
In a coitus with letters!
The slug chafes on the stone's dryness.
It drips over the aridness of the desert that is the life of a stone.
It screws the stone.
The slug requires this desert to live.

11.

That the word "wall" not be a symbol
of obstacles to freedom
of repressed desires
of childhood restrictions,
etcetera (those things the explorers find
in the disclosures of mental arcana).
No.
The wall that allures me
is made of tiles, adobe applied
to the abdomen of a house.
I have a crawling taste
for going through entryways
coming down into the cracks in walls
through fissures, through crevices–lascivious as ivy.
To be the tile's blind lip.
The worm that glows.

12.

His France is useless.
It's only good for playing violin.
From drinking water out of a hat the ants already know who
    he is.
It's totally useless.
The same as saying:
a dust that likes what's left of the soup is a fly.
He said one needs to be a nobody his whole life.
To be a developed nothing.
He said the origin of the artist is in this act of suicide.

13.

Place where there is decadence.
In which the houses begin to die and bats inhabit them.
In which the grasses enter, enter men, houses shut from
    the inside.
The moonlight will find only rocks vagabonds dogs.
Grounds besieged by abandon, given over to poverty.
Where men will have the strength of poverty.
And the ruins will bear fruit.

Portrait

As a child, he lengthened rivers.
He walked slowly, obscurely—half-formed
in silence.
He wanted to be the voice in which stones speak.
Landscapes wandered across his eyes.
His chants were full of fountains.
Like an aroma, he stuck to things.

An Education on Invention

> The things that don't exist are more beautiful.
> —Felisdônio

I

To touch the intimacies of the world it's essential to know:

    a) that the splendor of a morning doesn't open with a fork
    b) how violets prepare a day for its death
    c) why red-stripe butterflies are so devoted to tombstones
    d) that a man who spies his existence in the campfire will be saved
    e) that a river flowing between two hyacinths bears more tenderness than one that runs between two lizards
    f) how to assume the voice of a fish
    g) which side of the night will dampen first
etc.
etc.
etc.
Unlearning eight hours a day teaches such principles.

II

To uninvent objects.
The comb, for example.
To give the comb abilities of not combing.
Until it is left with the inclination to be a begonia.
Or a *gravanha*.

To use some words until they belong to no language.

III

To repeat and repeat—until altered.
To repeat is a gift for flare.

IV

In The Treaty of the Grandeurs of the Lowly it was written:

Poetry is when the afternoon is adept with dahlias.
When day sleeps earlier next to a bird.
When man invents his first gecko.
When the intersection takes over the night.
And a frog swigs the sunrise.

V

Carrier ants enter the house with their backsides first.

VI

Things without names are better pronounced by children.

VII

In the undoing was the verb.
Only after did I see its delirium.
The verb's delirium was at the beginning, where the child says:
I hear the birds' ache.
The child doesn't know the verb to hear
doesn't work for colors, only sound.
So he changes its function and gets delirious.
And that's all there is.
What's the sound of a poet, what's the sound
of a new birth?
A verb has to jumpstart delirium.

VIII

To enter the state of being a tree, it's necessary
to begin with a gecko's amphibian torpor
at three in the afternoon in the month of August.

In two years, inertia and scrub grass will begin
to expand our mouths. We will suffer
a little lyrical decomposition
until the scrub grass emerges in our speech.

For now, I've designed the smell of the trees.

IX

A stone's silence is heightless.

X

Nature getting sick from us:
injecting affliction into stone.
(As Rodin did.)

XI

To take verbal proximities from an open space
is the same as taking a fly from an asylum
and giving it a bath.
It's a practice without pain.
It's like being dawned by a flock of birds.
Any vegetal defect on a bird can modify
its twittering.

XII

Things no longer want to be seen
by reasonable people:
They want to be seen in blue—
to be the child you stare at bird-like.

XIII

Poetry is to flap without wings.

XIV

Semantic blocks provide equilibrium. Where
The abstract enters, grip it with wire. Beside the primal
leave a gentle scholar. Apply a swelling
to the dryness. Park some shit with the sublime.
And no reason to sanctify the dirty penis.

from The Book about Nothing

Ants

I didn't need to read Saint Paul, Saint Augustine,
Saint Jerome, or Thomas of Aquinas,
not even Saint Francis of Assisi—
to arrive at God.
Ants showed him to me.

(I have a doctorate in ants.)

The Book about Nothing

It's easier to make a gift from folly than from good sense.

-

Everything I don't invent is false.

-

There are many serious ways to say nothing, but only poetry is true.

-

What has the most presence in me is what I'm missing.

-

The best way I found to know myself was doing the opposite.

-

I am very prepared from such conflicts.

-

It's impossible for the mouth to be absent in language: no words stay abandoned from the being that revealed them.

-

My dawn is going to open at dusk.

-

Better than naming is eluding. Verse doesn't need to give notions.

•

My reverse is more visible than a front post.

•

The wise man is the one who guesses.

•

To have more certainty I have to know more imperfections.

•

Inertia is my principal act.

•

I don't come out from inside myself, not even to fish.

•

Wisdom might be conversion into a tree.

•

Style is an abnormal mode of expression: it's a stigma.

•

Fish don't have honors or horizontals.

•

Whenever I have a desire to count things up, I do nothing; but when I don't have a desire to count anything, I make poetry.

•

I wanted to be read by stones.

•

Words hide me without much care.

•

Wherever I am not words find me.

•

There are histories so true that at times it seems they are invented.

•

A word opened the dresser for me. She wanted me to be her.

•

Literary therapy consists of abandoning language to the point that it may express our undermost desires.

•

I want the word that fits in the beak of a small bird.

•

This task of ceasing is what pushes my sentences to come before me.

•

The atheist is a person capable of proving scientifically that he isn't nothing. He will only compare himself to the saints. And the saints want to be God's worms.

•

Better than arriving at nothing is to discover something true.

•

The artist is nature's error. Beethoven was a perfect error.

•

It is purity that makes me impure.

•

Whiteness corrupts me.

•

I don't like the word *accustomed*.

•

My difference is always less.

•

The poetic word must approach the level of humor to be serious.

•

I don't need an ending to arrive.

•

From the place where I am I've already left.

Desiring to Be

1.

With pieces of Manoel I assemble an astonished being.

2.

I prefer crooked lines, like God. As a boy, I dreamed of having a shorter leg (only so that I'd be able to meander in a crooked line). I saw the old pharmacist in the afternoon, climbing the ladder in his alley, crooked and deserted . . . clip clop, clip clop. He had distinction.

If I'd possessed a shorter leg, the whole world would have had to watch me: there goes the crooked boy climbing the ladder in the alley clip clop, clip clop.

I would have had distinction. The very sanctification of I.

3.

It isn't bragging when I explain
        I have no splendor
I'm more concerned with rust
        than with luster
I work hard to do the unnecessary.
What's practical has no verification,
        but the impractical is different.
I'm no longer a man who suffers from grandeur.
Only low-lying things make me star-like.
I get twitchy for idleness.
It's violets that enlarge me.

4.

I write an archaic Manoel-esque idiolect (Idiolect is the dialect idiots use to speak to the walls and with the flies.) I need to upset meanings. Purposeless is healthier than solemnity. (To cleanse a certain solemnity from words, I use manure.) I'm very hygienic. The cerebral touches in my writing are just a precaution to avoid succumbing to the temptation to make myself less foolish than others. I am highly regarded for my foolishness. Of this I deliver certainty.

Footnote: On archaic speech: I enjoy an orthographic wandering in pursuit of the archaic. Stomachus for stomach. Pandæmonium for pandemonium. A pleasure perhaps for what's left behind. A more fossilized memory. For me, to hear "stomachus" stirs an atavistic resonance. A thing that dreams of retro-ways.

5.

I'm a subject full of hiding places.
Lofts give me constancy.
When there's time, I read the maidenhairs of a fern.
If there's time, Proust.
I listen to birds and Beethoven.
I like Bola Sete and Charlie Chaplin.

The day is going to die wide open in me.

6.

I transport my origins in a bier.
My voice has an addiction to fountains.
I want to advance to the beginning.
To arrive at the infancy of words.
Where they still urinate on your leg.
Before any hands can model their use.
As a child scribbles a verb for what he's missing.
I want to stick to the silky yarn of sound.
To be the voice of the hidden lizard.
To trigger an unveiling of the arcane.

7.

I know assembling disconnections is a way out of madness.
I'm a product of such failed encounters.
Good sense absurds me.
Verbal delirium is my medication.
To give joy to the sewers (language accepts everything).
(And I know that Baudelaire spent many months feeling
uneasy at his inability to think of a title for his poems.
A title that could harmonize its conflicts. Until *Fleurs
du mal* appeared. Beauty and the aching. This antithesis
reassured him).

Antitheses can sanctify.

8.

I was born to administer the random
       the futile
       the useless

I belong as a maker of images.
I operate by similarities, by extracting
what's similar between people and trees
       people and frogs
       people and rocks
       etcetera.

Similarities between trees and myself.
I don't have much capacity for clarity.
I strive for a vegetable wisdom.
(Vegetable wisdom for finding a frog on the stalk of a plant.
And when possessed by stone,
  I'll develop a mineral wisdom as well.)

9.

Maybe science can classify and name the organs in a thrush
but it can't measure its pleasure.
Science can't calculate the horsepower
in the pleasure of a thrush.

To accumulate vast amounts of information
is to lose the magic wand that is a guess—I guess.

The thrushes guess.

10.

I think of the fly clinging to the side of a drain
as more momentous than a strung jewel.

Of the tiny coverings Egyptians made for bird mummies as
 more momentous
than Tutankhamen's sarcophagus.

The man who gave up on life out of feeling like a sewer
I think of as more earth-shattering than a nuclear plant.

Things without dimension are important.
Thus the bird *tu-you-you* is more important for its pronouns
than for the size to which it grows.

It's in the lowly I see exuberance.

11.

I prefer machines that aren't intended to function:
when they're full of sand, ants, and moss—
which may one day alchemize into flowers.

(Objects without function are more intimate with neglect.)

The same for discarded latrines, excellent for keeping crickets—
which may one day alchemize into violets.

(I'm overpious when it comes to violets.)

It is the things given to neglect that draw me to God.
Lord, I'm proud of the useless!

(Neglect protects me.)

12.

I saw a nail from the 13th century
half-buried in a 3 x 4 wall, white,
in the 23rd São Paulo Art Biennial in 1994.
I studied this nail awhile.
What remained to be decided was this: if the rusted object
would be the same if it were from 13th century as from the 12th.
It was a lone nail and indisputable.
It could be an announcement about solitude.
A nail is an indisputable thing.

13.

I come from noblemen who turned poor.
The fortune of haughtiness was left to me.
With this illness of grandeur,
I have to monumentalize insects!
(Christ monumentalized Humility when he kissed the feet
   of his disciples.)
Saint Frances monumentalized the birds.
Vieira, the fish.
Shakespeare—Love, Doubt, the fools.
Charlie Chaplin monumentalized the vagabond.
With this mania for grandeur
I have to monumentalize the poor things of the ground,
   pissed on by the dew.

14.

What I don't know how to construct I unbuild in phrases.

To make the nothing appear.

(What it demonstrates is that man is a dark well.
From here, above, one can't see that nothing.
But when you arrive at the bottom of the well, there it is.)

To lose that nothing is an impoverishment.

1998 - 2009

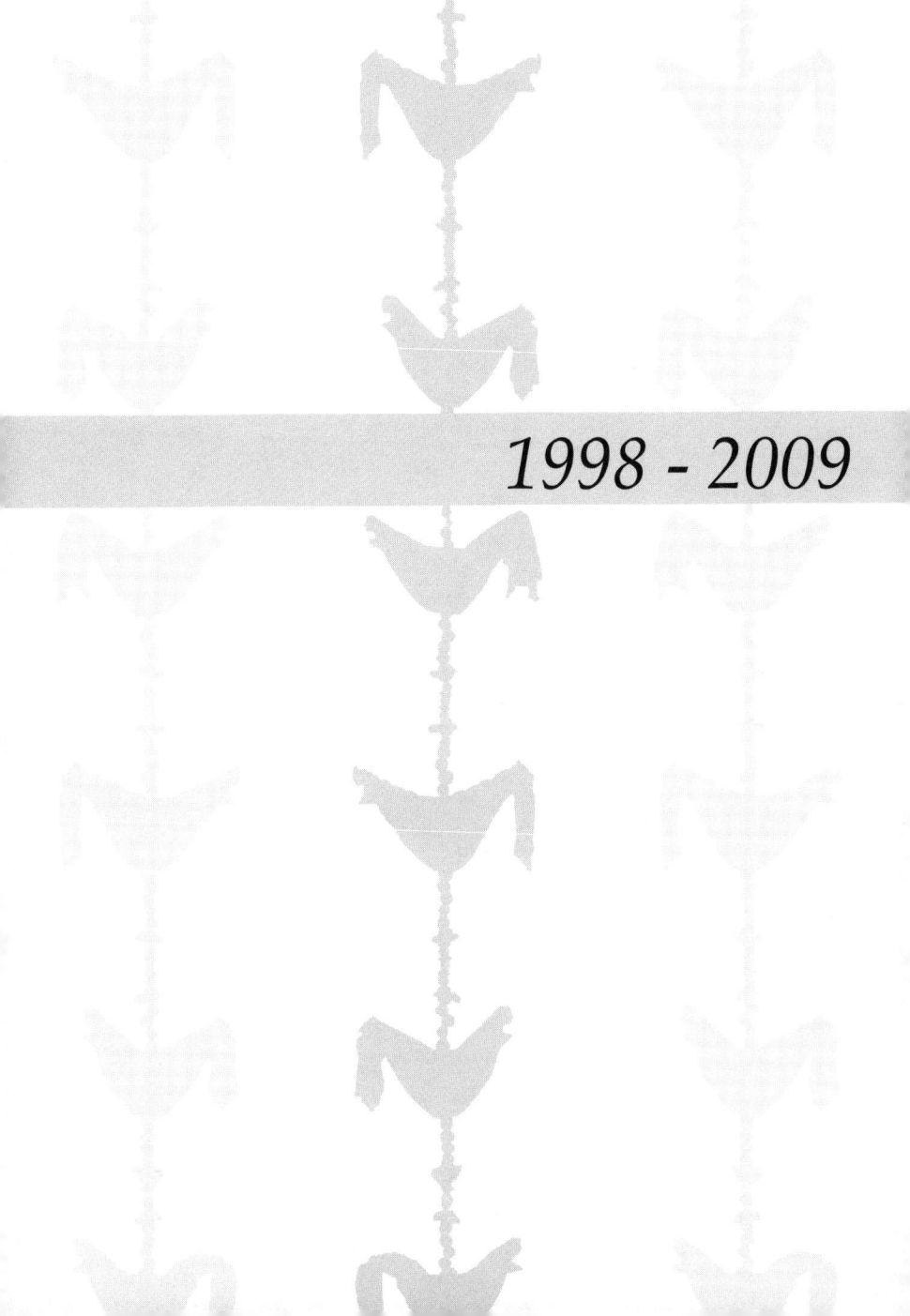

In War

The Mayor dispatched a messenger by horse with a letter to the Emperor.

The letter announced the city had been invaded by Paraguayan troops and expressed a need for extra recourses.

Two months later, the messenger handed the letter to the Emperor.

When the recourses arrived, the Paraguayans were no longer there.

The Emperor's men came with fifteen young women and a few provisions to eat on the way.

I guess they ate them all.

Corumbá is a city whose population is well mixed with Paraguayans.

Of Birds

To compose a treaty on birds
it's first necessary to have a river
with a few palms along its margins.
And within the yards of the homes
at the very least a few guava trees.
And swamps nearby, and the delicacies of swamps.
And it's key to have insects for the birds.
Tree insects above all, which are the most palatable.
The presence of dragonflies is desirable.
And the color blue is key in the life of a bird
as prior to being beautiful
a bird should be eternal.
A Bach fugue.

The Rock

Being a rock
I have the pleasure of lying on the ground.
I deprive no one but lizards and butterflies.
Certain shells take shelter in me.
Mosses grow from my interstices.
Birds use me to sharpen their beaks.
Sometimes a heron occupies me all day
and I feel praised.
There are other privileges to being a rock:
   a-I irritate the silence of insects.
   b-Am the beat of moonlight in solitude.
   c-In the mornings I soak in dew.
   d-And the sun compliments me first.

Portrait of the Artist as a Thing

There's a vegetal heat in the artist's voice.
He'll have to make his language cross-eyed
to get to the water's whisper in the leaves.

He'll never have the inclination again
to reflect on things.
He'll have the inclination to be them.
He won't have ideas anymore: he'll have rain, afternoons,
wind, the flap of birds . . .
Where the flies govern over the crumbs from lunch,
he'll think: desertion.
The torque of words
will extract it from within him.

It'll come out drunk from having been.
It'll come out drunk and bleak. Seeing leeches
twisted, fat, pinned
to the horse's stomach—
the child goes and carves them out:
the horse's dark blood runs.

The artist has to drain
that darker substance.
To arrive sick from grief,
his limitations and defeats.
He has to make his language cross-eyed
to the point of perceiving the sun's perfume
in the heron's eye.

Invented Memoir

I leaned into the morning the way a bird leans and a vision appeared: the afternoon running behind a dog. I was fourteen. This vision must have come from my origins. I don't remember ever seeing a dog outrun the afternoon. I made a note of it anyway. Such leaps of the imagination are what make our speech more beautiful. I made a note in a phrasebook. By this point, I was already saving visions like this one. I had another that month, but first I should tell you the circumstances. I transported parts of my childhood between the kitchen wall and the yard. I pretended to put a yoke on the frogs behind our kitchen. We understood each other well. I fixed things so the frog's skin matched the color of the ground. It seemed right, since they were of the ground and grimy. One day I said to my mother: A frog is a piece of the ground that jumps. She said I was mixed up, that a frog isn't a piece of the ground. Now that I'm older, I think of the prophet Jeremiah. He was so distraught at seeing his Zion destroyed and dragged through the fire that a vision came to him in his home: even the stones in the street were crying. Later, calmer, writing to a friend, he remembered the vision: even the stones in the street had cried. It was such a beautiful sentence because there was no reason in it. He said this.

from Song of Seeing

Having lived many years in the scrub grass in the way of birds
The boy took on a bird's kind of stare—
He obtained a fountain-esque vision.
He observed things the way birds observed them.
All the unnamed things.
Water wasn't the word water yet.
Rock wasn't the word rock.
They just were.
Words were free of grammar and could inhabit any position.
So it was the boy could inaugurate them as he pleased.
He could give rocks the costume of the sun.
He could give song the sun's format.
And, if he wanted to end up a bee, it was only a matter
of opening the word bee
and stepping inside it.
As if it were the infancy of language.

from Biography of Dew

The supreme wealth of man is his incompleteness.
In this regard I am affluent.
Words that accept me as I am—I can't accept.
I can't bear to be merely a subject who opens doors,
pulls valves, looks at his watch, buys bread
at six in the afternoon, steps outside, sharpens
his pencil, considers the grape, etcetera.

Forgive me, but I need
to be Others, to bolster man
with butterflies.

The Illness

I never lived far from my country.
Yet I suffer from farness.
In my childhood my mother had the illness.
She's the one who gave it to me.
Later my father went to work at a place
that gave this illness to people.
It was a place without a name or neighbors.
People said it was the nail on the toe at the end of the world.
We grew up with no other houses nearby.
A place that offered only birds, trees, a river and its fish.
There were unbridled horses in the scrub grass,
their backs covered in butterflies.
The rest was distance.
Distance was an empty thing we carried in the eye,
what my father called exile.

Self-Portrait

At birth, I wasn't awake and didn't see
the hour.
This was eons ago.
It was on the bank of a river.
I've already died fourteen times.
Only the last remains.
I wrote fourteen books
and from them I'm unleashed.
They're all repetitions of the first.
(I can pretend to be others, but can't escape too far.)
I planted eighteen trees, but could be four.
In thought and letters, I loved ninety girls,
but could be nine.
I produced un-objects, thirty-five
or could be eleven.
Let me cite the most worn: a milky scissor,
a dawn opener, a buckle
for fastening silences, a tack that crackles,
a velvet screw, etc. I have a confession:
ninety percent of what I write
is invention; only ten percent is a lie.
I want to die on the mounded bank of a river—
without flies in my emptied mouth.

The Art of Infantilizing Ants

1.

Things had a poetic uselessness for us.
Our unknowing was everything in the backyard.
We invented a trick for making games out of words.
The trick was to be absurd.
Like saying: I hung a bird from a cloud . . .
Or as Bugrinha said: a made-up river poured through our house.
Or as Grandfather said: a grasshopper's gaze is without
    principles.
Mano Preto asked: Did they make the hummingbird small
so that it could fly standing erect?
The distances made us add up to less.
Father used to work the land work the land.
Mother made candles.
My brother would saddle frogs.
Bugrinha beat a stick against the body of a frog and it turned
    to stone.

2.

Father lived at the end of a place.
Here is a lacuna of people, he said:
it only almost has a swallow and tree.
What pushes dawn's button is the Piping-guan.
One day an official doctor appeared full of suspenders and manners.
On the bank of the swamp, hawk-crabbers went on feasting on their crabs.
The same distance lay between the frogs and the fields.
People joked with the earth.
When the doctor appeared, he said: you need to do something about your hookworm.
Near us there was always a waiting of Ruddy Doves.
The doctor hated Ruddy Doves.

3.

At the table the doctor announced:
you're the happy ones because you live in this empire.
My father spat this empire to the side.
The doctor spoke a curious kind of nonsense.
Mano Preto took advantage: a cricket is a useless being when it comes to silence.
Mano Preto didn't have a personal entity, only as a thing.
(Would that be a defect of God?)
We spoke our nonsense as a joke, but the doctor spoke it with seriousness.
Father snatched the joke from us.
It's the dark that makes you sparkle.
Bugrinha stood open-mouthed.

4.

Every month or so a peddler's cart appeared, pulled by four herds of bulls at the end of that place. The cart came bearing caramels, biscuits, combs, snare rings, Micravel extract, pieces of white cotton for making skirts, mosquito netting, bottles of arnica to cure bruises, earrings made of *peschibeque* seed—so many things without sanctity . . .

My mother bought arnica and biscuits.
Doña Maria, Lara's wife, bought earrings and Micravel extract.

My grandfather supplied abandon.

Of everything, what would remain for us was a feeling of a thing forgotten in the land—a pencil in a peninsula.

The Two

I'm two beings, really.
The first is fruit of the love between João and Alice.
The second is of letters: fruit of a nature
that thinks in images, as Valéry put it.
The first you can observe in terms of nails, shirts, my hat and
    vanities.
The second in letters, syllables, these vain sentences.
And we accept that when you extend your love it is to both of us.

Filth

I prefer the bleak words that live in the corners
of kitchens—filth, grit, tin cans—
over those that live in fraternities—
words like excellence, prominent, majestic.
My alter egos are filth and grit, the devils
who hole up in kitchen corners—
Ones like Seven Ball, Mário the Frog Catcher,
Luisa Leather Reins, etc.
All of them drunk and strange.
All of them grubby and in rags.
One day someone suggested to me I adopt
a respectable alter ego—a prince,
admiral, or senator.
But who, I asked,
would dwell in my empty corners
if these devils don't?

Resigned

No longer can I dodge the hot sand
like a tiny fish escaped from a hook.
No longer can I run in the rain the way calves run.
No longer can I somersault in the wind.
Now
I spend my hours playing with words.
Carnival play.
Today I tied my mask on a word's face.
I do what I can.

Invented Memoir, II

My mother gave me a river.
It was my birthday and she didn't know what to give.
It had been awhile since the peddler came by that forgotten place.
If the peddler had come by she would've bought candy or a tin of cookies.
But the peddler didn't come by so I got the river.
The same river that had always passed behind our house.
I liked the gift more than if it had been candy from the peddler.
My brother pouted, he liked the river as well.
Our mother promised him he'd get a tree for his birthday.
A tree covered in birds.
I heard this promise and thought it was fine.
The birds would spend the day on the banks of my river.
At night, they'd sleep in my brother's tree.
My brother teased that his present got flowers in September.
And a river doesn't get flowers!
I told him a tree doesn't get piranhas.
What united us was swimming naked in the river with the herons.
In this regard, our life was a caress.

About the Author

Manoel de Barros, author of more than twenty collections of poetry, was born in the wetlands region of Brazil known as the Pantanal in 1916. His unusual life and work were the subject of Joel Pizzini's 1989 film *O Caramujo Flor*. He has received Brazil's highest awards for poetry multiple times: the Jabuti Prize in both 1990 and 2002, the Nestle Poetry Prize in 1997 and 2006, and the Ministry of Culture's Cecilia Meireles Prize in 1998. His poetry has been translated into French, German, and Spanish; this collection is the first translation of his work to appear in English.

About the Translator

Idra Novey's first book of poems, *The Next Country*, was selected for the Kinereth Gensler Award and released in 2008 with Alice James Books. She received a PEN Translation Fund Award for her translations of Brazilian poet Paulo Henriques Britto, *The Clean Shirt of It* (BOA Editions, 2007) and a National Endowment for the Arts Fellowship for her translations of Manoel de Barros. She currently teaches in the School of the Arts at Columbia University and serves as director of Columbia's Center for Literary Translation.